UNEXPLAINABLE

Inspirational Stories of God's Love
in the Most Unique Ways

Ashley Carter

ISBN 979-8-89130-006-4 (paperback)
ISBN 979-8-89130-007-1 (digital)

Christian Faith Publishing
832 Park Avenue
Meadville, PA 16335
www.christianfaithpublishing.com

Printed in the United States of America

Dedication

This book is dedicated to all of the wonderful people that I get to call family!

To my loving and supportive husband,
    You have been my rock, my confidant, and my greatest cheerleader. Your unwavering belief in me has fueled my dreams and aspirations. This book is a testament to the love and strength you've provided throughout our journey together.

To my two children, of whom I am so proud,
    You are the reason I strive for greatness every day. Your resilience, kindness, and unwavering support have been a constant source of inspiration. May this book serve as a reminder of the love and pride I hold for each of you.

To my wonderful grandchildren,

Your laughter and boundless energy light up my world. You remind me of the beauty in simplicity and the importance of cherishing every moment. This book is dedicated to you, with the hope that it will inspire your own dreams and adventures.

To my parents,

From the very beginning, you instilled in me the values of hard work, determination, and the importance of following my heart. Your love and encouragement have been my guiding stars. This book is a tribute to the foundation you've provided and the enduring love you've shown.

To my brother,

Your unwavering strength, determination, and indomitable spirit have been a beacon of inspiration in my life. Your ability to face challenges head-on, never giving up, has shown me the true meaning of resilience. You've taught me that no matter how tough the journey may be, we can overcome any obstacle with unwavering determination.

This book is dedicated to you, my dear brother, with the deepest gratitude for being my source of strength and a constant reminder that dreams are worth chasing, challenges are worth conquering, and giving up is never an option.

Thank you

First and foremost, I want to express my gratitude to God, the very reason I have stories to share with you. Without his divine guidance and blessings, this book of short stories would not have been possible.

To my family, your unwavering support and love have been my anchor throughout this journey. You've been there in every chapter of my life, and your encouragement has meant the world to me.

To my friends, thank you for your encouragement, laughter, and shared moments that have enriched my life and shaped my perspective. Your presence is a treasure.

To my church community, your faith and fellowship have provided me with strength and inspiration. Your prayers and support have meant more than words can express.

I extend my heartfelt appreciation to 1819 News for the incredible opportunities they have given me.

It's an honor to work with such a dedicated and talented team.

And last but certainly not least, I want to give a special thank you to Annie Holmquist, a remarkable journalist and a dear friend. Your mentorship, wisdom, and unwavering belief in my writing have been invaluable. You are the best, and I am deeply grateful for your guidance.

This book is a reflection of the love, support, and opportunities I've been blessed with. Each word on these pages is a testament to the kindness and generosity of those who have touched my life and to the many blessings from God. Thank you from the bottom of my heart.

With immense gratitude,

Ashley

Choose Life

I was a senior in high school, eighteen years old, making big plans for my future with no idea what was up ahead for me.

I have struggled with the thought of actually telling my story, but I strongly believe that there is someone out there that will be better off knowing that they aren't alone. Many have been where I was and have been faced with the same choice.

I will never forget. It was spring break of my senior year, and I normally didn't go anywhere, but a close family friend was going to the beach, and my parents decided to let me go. I had just broken up with the guy I had been dating and needed to remove myself from being anywhere near him, and this was the perfect way.

We had only been there for maybe a day or two, and I began to get very sick. I had no idea what was going on, but I knew something was off. I called my parents and decided to drive back home. Long story short, I ended up in the emergency room scheduled for surgery to remove my gallbladder.

Of course, the surgery was postponed due to the discovery that I was actually pregnant. I honestly can't explain the feelings that came over me. Of course, I was scared and nervous. I remember how caring my parents and my grandparents were and the precious little lamb they bought me from the hospital gift shop.

There was never any discussion of doing anything other than what we did next. We started preparing for the future and became excited about the sweet blessing that God had chosen to give me. I did notify the biological father with whom I had recently ended the relationship, but he had other plans for his future, and being a dad wasn't one at that time.

Being a senior in high school, almost everyone close to me or somewhat a friend, told me that I shouldn't have to do that alone. I heard all of the arguments from them. The constant trying to reason that I was so young and would be alone and needed to live my life. It didn't take long for me to block it out. I knew that there were two of us now, not just one. It was our lives, not just mine.

My parents were a huge blessing and walked through it daily with me. The doctor appointments, listening to the heartbeat, and seeing him for the first time growing in me were emotionally overwhelming. I already loved him more than anything! I couldn't fathom the thought of him not being there.

I know that not everyone has a support system like I did, but we are a lot stronger than we realize. God ordained my steps and prepared me for the journey. He already knew what was going to happen, and all I had to do was trust Him. It was hard most days, but I did. He blessed me with this awesome guy, who is now my husband and has been with me since I was four months into my pregnancy. He was there when my son was born and is the best father!

If you or someone you know is going through this, there is hope! You are not alone. The beautiful blessing of a child is the greatest gift. My son, who is soon to be twenty-two years old, is such a blessing, and his hugs seem to solve all the world's problems.

Isn't it funny how God knew that's just what I needed?

Choose life! Choose love!

The Oak Tree

There once sat a tall oak tree on the very top of the property owned by my family. I distinctly remember it as a child. It was tall and majestic—one of those things you could never forget. My grandparents had farmed the land and kept it up, so while there for the summers, I spent many days around that tree.

To be honest, as a child, I never thought much of it. It was big and beautiful, but other than that, it was just a tree. As I grew older and many years passed, the land changed and my grandparents became older and farming slowed down. The one constant that never changed was the tree.

At one point, my uncle began to raise cattle on the land, and I didn't visit it as often. I started to forget about the tree—after all, it was just a tree, and I didn't think at the time it would be very significant in my life.

As time passed on, I grew older and began to date. In those dating years, I met a few bad apples. I learned some hard lessons and matured. The older I got, the more my "list" changed. I remember writing down all the things that I wanted in a future husband. Tall, dark, handsome, maybe a doctor, and the list goes on.

In the spring of 2001, I was introduced to a fella. I didn't think much of it at the time. He checked off the boxes, except for being a doctor, though he was in college and working toward a degree in the medical field. It didn't take long until I was falling for him.

We had gone on dates and talked for hours on the phone. We talked about life and plans and all the normal things. I knew at the time there was something different about him. I just couldn't put my finger on it. It was like we were meant to be together. God had strategically planned this. The way we met, the things we went through together. It was all a part of a greater plan.

I, like any other young lady, needed some type of confirmation. I remember one day he took me to visit his parents. They had a beautiful piece of property, and his mom loved to get out and walk it, so we did just that. She showed me everything, and we talked and walked until we stopped at the top of the property. I remember looking up and seeing this tall oak tree on the property that joined at the back.

I looked over at them and told them how familiar that tree looked to me. It reminded me so much of the one from my family's property I had spent so much time around as a child. I knew my family's property was close by, but there was no way that could be it. I asked his mom who owned the property, and she told me that the gentleman had at one time had cattle on it and she would actually feed them.

I began to ask more questions until it finally hit me. This was my family's property, and that was the tree. There was just one thing left to do. I still had an aunt that lived on the property, so over the fence, we went, and the journey began there.

I was looking for a sign, and I got it. Not only had God divinely planned our meeting, but He also had already joined our families together before we had even met. We actually spent the first few years of our marriage living right by the oak tree and raising two little kids.

Now after twenty-one years of marriage filled with a few hard times, sleepless nights, busy lives, and lots of love and forgiveness, our marriage, much like that tall oak tree, is still standing.

The Dinner Table

The age-old tradition of gathering around the dinner table is about so much more than eating. Sitting together without any distractions and having real conversations is something that we all could use a little more of.

I don't know about you, but I can remember a time that we would spend with family around a long dining table filled with the best southern cooking you could ever imagine. The smell would greet you at the door and so would my family with a wonderful warm embrace.

The conversations, the laughs, the smiles, the siblings kicking each other under the table, and the one rather firm debate would always be guaranteed. Time would literally seem to stand still and nothing else mattered. Everything outside of those moments could wait.

It seems as though this tradition is one that many are not honoring anymore. I was reminded of how important it really is the other day when my twenty-two-year-old son commented at lunch. He said, "It's not about what's on the table or what table we are at, it matters that we are here sitting together as a family." Wow!

I know that lives are busy and sometimes it is not always possible to sit and dine together for every meal, but setting aside time to do this when it is possible is vitally important. Putting away our phones and any outside distractions and just focusing on each other and sharing the moment is not only a time of bonding but also a time of healing and helping each other.

Every day we are faced with decisions and deadlines. There are many things that need to be done, whether it be at home or at your job. The time we spend sitting and talking at dinner is time that we can completely take ourselves away from those distractions and really focus on each other.

The world would love us to continue to live in the monotonous mundane life of a robot, never looking up to see what is really going on around us. God, however, blessed us with a beautiful world to explore and enjoy. He blessed us with family and friends and gives us time every day to enjoy those things.

The benefits of gathering together and actually listening to each other can bring you so much more joy than a stranger's social media feed which actually probably isn't as awesome as you think it is.

Take a moment to enjoy real life, the life you have been blessed with. Learn to step away from the outside world and into the lives of your family and friends. Our family needs this, our friends need this and our world definitely needs this. Time is precious and it is short.

Break bread together and enjoy all the blessings and little moments that can't be replaced.

I Remember, but I Think Some of Us Forgot

As a little girl, I can remember looking forward to the summertime. I remember the smell of breakfast being cooked in the kitchen by my grandmother or *Nanny* as I called her. She was up around five in the morning to fix a full spread for PawPaw to eat before he left for work. I remember it was ready right before he sat down to eat. I remember the look I got before he left and the reminder to behave.

Most of all, I remember that he was no wimp. I am sure that some of that toughness came from his time in the Army. He worked from sunrise to sunset without one word of complaint. He actually owned a steel company, and as a kid, I really thought he was made of steel. His words meant something, and he took others very seriously. If there was a problem, he fixed it. He didn't call someone else. I remember that the dinner table was prepared before he arrived home from work, and we sat down to eat together.

I remember that during the day, Nanny and I worked in the garden and ran any errands that needed to be done. I remember watching Nanny canning things and her letting me help. I think my favorite memory was what we did on the weekends. I remember riding on the tire cover of the tractor as my PawPaw worked the garden. I remember gathering vegetables and snapping beans.

I remember that my other grandfather, *Poppy*, carried that same work ethic. I don't think he retired until he was eighty years old. I remember that there wasn't an instrument that he couldn't play, and he didn't just play it. He made you want to listen for hours. I remember that my Memaw was just as thoughtful to fix breakfast and dinner for Poppy, and she even brought him his plate first. Their love story is one right out of the Bible. Poppy was not a talker, but he didn't have to speak for you to know his character or what he stood for.

I remember watching these things as a little girl, but my fear is that there won't be someone like me again. There won't be a little girl that remembers life this way. There won't be a little girl who remembers that men were men of their word. There won't be those who never wavered in their beliefs. There won't be strong men of honor to handle things and keep our world from continuing to go crazy. I pray that I am wrong. I pray that men will stand up stronger than ever before and that the women behind them will have dinner ready when they get home. I pray their grandkids will enjoy the same things I enjoyed.

I pray that where we are now is not where we want to stay. I remember that what I learned by watching all of this growing up was that it continued in my family. My dad works just like his dad and so on. I remember the things my grandparents taught me, but one of the most important was to not give up ever. If we are ever going to get back to times like this, then we need strong men and supportive women to come together and fight back.

Let's not bury our heads in the sand. Let's do what we can so that our kids will remember.

The Watch

I am often questioned about the vintage watch that is always worn on my right wrist. Some are intrigued by the way it looks. It does seem to have a sense of sweet, dainty Southern charm to it. I love it for all of those reasons as well, but that is not my reason for wearing it every day.

I love when friends ask, "Does it actually work?" I reply that it works for me. This watch is actually the only piece of jewelry that was given to me that belonged to my Nanny. I make a point to wear it daily as a reminder to me of her and all the things she meant to me.

I have often thought about having it repaired so that it actually serves its purpose of telling time. However, for me, it is serving a bigger purpose in reminding me of a certain time—a time when life was a bit simpler. A time when families sat down and shared stories around the dinner table. A time when time was all we had, and there was no rush.

I find myself looking down at it a lot. The time is still set at 1:44, and I wonder what she was doing at the time. Was she canning vegetables? Was she cleaning up after a big lunch gathering on a Sunday afternoon? Was she outside on the porch shelling peas? Or maybe she was tending to her rose bushes.

There is something very special about wearing something that she wore and remembering who she was. She was exactly who I wanted to be when I grew up and became a grandmother. I wanted to treat my grandchild to a day in the garden. I wanted to teach them about life—more importantly about God and how to treat others. I wanted to take them into "town," as she would say, for a chocolate-dipped cone from Dairy Queen. My nanny treated me to these things very often.

I learned a lot from Nanny. I learned things you can't be taught in a classroom or a conference room and most of her life lessons came straight from the bible and always a scripture to back it up. I learned about life, working hard, and fighting for what you believe in.

I know to some, this watch may not work like the world thinks it should, but that seems to be the problem these days. Maybe we need to stop, like this watch, and take a breath. Take a moment to enjoy the little things and the little moments that turn into memories. I will continue to wear my watch just the way it is and be thankful for everything my Nanny is still teaching me through it. It works just perfectly for me.

Chicken and Dumplings

The Secret Ingredient (Love!)

Memaw's kitchen, with the smell of love and hard work, greeted you as soon as you came in the door. Every holiday or special occasion, we knew we could look forward to a big pot full of goodness known as chicken and dumplings. She would even make them special for us if we were sick and nothing seemed to be hitting the spot. I don't think there has ever been anything that quite compares.

There isn't a single person who has had my Memaw's famous chicken and dumplings and didn't ask for more. Honestly, have you ever tasted one certain food that solved all your problems or everything that had gone wrong before you ate it? It's true comfort food.

As all of the grandchildren, especially the girls, began to grow up, we wanted to learn how to cook them and find out what made them taste so good. I remember several occasions when we would all get together and watch Memaw start cooking from scratch. We watched every little detail and all of the ingredients that went in.

After many times of watching and helping her, I tried to make them on my own. They just didn't taste the same. I knew that I had followed her recipe exactly as she had said. I couldn't quite figure out what I had done wrong.

It finally dawned on me: Memaw was missing. She was the only thing that wasn't there while I was cooking. It began to occur to me that not only did she work hard to make those for us, but she also must have been pouring in all of her love while cooking.

Once my grandson was born, I wanted to be sure that Memaw shared that same memory of cooking with him. We took a day, and my daughter, Memaw, myself, and the little fella spent time in the kitchen. We laughed, made a mess, told stories, and took turns holding my grandson. I quickly realized that I never wanted to have dumplings without her.

Grandmothers have a special way of making everything feel better and obviously taste better. My

Memaw does just that. We are so fortunate to have her still with us and making these memories mean more than gold.

I am still learning to make dumplings taste like hers, and I seem to be getting better each time. I have learned to be still and enjoy cooking them and to think about the people I am preparing them for. I take a moment to pray and remember all the good memories shared with each one.

It may seem silly to some, but love is a huge part of life, and to leave it out of anything can change so much! Always share love, but love with truth, honor, forgiveness, and compassion. It may take a minute, but I promise that you will not regret it.

Being a Woman Is a Beautiful Thing

As a little girl, I remember the days spent playing in the backyard and the many evenings spent playing with my Barbie collection until dinner time. I would brush and braid their hair until it was just right. I may have driven my parents a bit crazy with all of the clothes and shoes that I just knew I needed to complete my collection.

On a typical Saturday, after completing my chores, I would love to go outside to the big fig trees in the backyard. I would take some of my mom's quilts and begin to drape them over the branches to make a little house. I would gather some branches with bigger leaves and tie them together to make a homemade broom and sweep the dirt until it was nice and smooth.

My friends and I would play out there for hours, maybe having a tea party or just giggling about silly things. Sometimes we would pretend we were different people in another place. Other times we would aggravate the neighbor. I think our continuous giggling might have disturbed her quiet Saturday plans. No matter what, we loved the little house we made.

I loved the beautiful dresses that I could get dressed up in for church on Sunday mornings and the pretty bows and ribbons that my mom would get to match them perfectly. The sound of the click/clack from my Sunday shoes on the tile floor was my favorite sound other than the Southern gospel music playing while getting ready.

Being a little girl was so much fun. I loved listening to Elvis with my mom and dancing in the living room. I loved cooking with my grandmother and playing dress-up with my granny. As I got older, I began to realize that all of the things that I loved doing came naturally to me. I loved holding the little babies, and I didn't mind taking care of the home and cooking. I enjoyed all of it and knew in my heart that I wanted to be a mom and have lots of little children.

Now as an adult, I see things changing. The nuclear family seems to be a thing of the past, and our children whose natural instincts are to be just what they were born to be, are daily influenced by the constantly created confusion. I, myself, walk into the store now and can't distinguish the women's section from the men's. Everything looks the same.

The natural yearning to feel the joy of being a wife and mother has now been replaced with modern-day feminism that would tell you those things are wrong and that what you really want is to be single and have a better career. It saddens me that so many have given in to that, and now the daily struggle with sadness or lack of true purpose never stops.

I would give anything to go back to being that little girl. Though time travel isn't an option, I can encourage those who have come after me to remember that their God-given natural instincts are not wrong. Don't be fooled by this world's constant attempt to confuse us. Don't become complacent and silent and allow this confusion to constantly be pushed into our faces. Remember that being a woman, naturally, is a beautiful thing. That's just the way God intended it to be.

Finding Joy in the Imperfections

I recently read a quote from Nancy Wilson, "Every woman has seasons when she's constantly behind. That's part of life, but focus on the importance of relationships in the home rather than the dirty dishes in the sink." I really wish I had read that in my twenties. It was so important to me as a young wife and mother that everything be in place in our home. Most days, that was never going to happen.

I remember feeling such disappointment in myself for not being able to accomplish all the things. At that time, all I could think about was all the laundry that needed to be done, the dishes that needed to be washed, and all the other household chores that needed to be completed. Now I wish I could go back and leave all of those things for later and jump in the mud puddles with my two toddlers, who were ever so eager to enjoy life.

I am sure that all of us go through this as we get older and start to understand that everything that our mothers told us really happens. There are regrets and moments in which you wish you could go back in time and have a do-over. Seeing as that isn't possible, we must press on and enjoy the present.

I honestly believe that it's only through learning lessons that we change our behavior. God has definitely taught me a few lessons along the way. Learning to see the little things and love the beauty in all things is one of them. Even the imperfect things bring me joy now. Of course, dirty dishes still bring on a sense of urgency but not in the way they used to.

Our homes are meant to be homes that are lived in, filled with joy and thanksgiving. They are meant to be a place of comfort and rest—a place where our husbands and children and even grandchildren come to feel safe and secure. Sure there may be toys lying around or maybe even that one sock that you just can't find the match for, but at the end of the day, did those things really matter?

I am learning that the things that we see as imperfections are not that at all. They are stories. They are real lives lived and moments that only happen once. Yes, the moment you're wearing your white shirt and that huge blob of ketchup lands right in the middle may seem like an imperfection, but maybe it was just a moment to allow you to laugh. I don't know about you, but laughter is needed more and more these days.

Take time to enjoy the opportunities to see the joy in the little imperfections that we call life. Love your family, read one more bedtime story, and laugh over the sink full of dishes that held the meal that fed your family. Maybe even let the littles wash them and enjoy the fun of cleaning up afterward. Life isn't meant to be perfect. It is meant to be lived.

The Joy of Motherhood

In the times we live in, there are more and more young women who seem to value fame and fortune above all else. They spend most of their days scrolling through social media, comparing themselves to the glamorous lives of influencers and celebrities.

Some single women may be intrigued by social media's message at first. They feel a sense of pressure to conform to society's expectations of successful women—to have a high-paying job, a perfect body, and a bustling social life. But as more research is done, it is easy to see that this message is a false depiction of what a young woman should aspire to be.

It's true that motherhood is challenging, but it's also one of the most rewarding and fulfilling experiences a woman can have. Being a mother means being a caretaker, a nurturer, and a source of unconditional love. It's a role that is both selfless and empowering.

Take a moment to think about all the amazing mothers in your life—your own mom, your grandmothers, and your friends and acquaintances who are raising children of their own. These women are some of the strongest, most resilient, and most compassionate people. God places those wonderful women in our lives to teach us and to help us to live uprightly.

In the end, the life depicted in the outside world and social media is not what God has truly called us to. It does require sacrifice, hard work, and patience, but we were born ready for the challenge. If we're honest, deep down, most of us women don't want to live a life like Chelsea Handler. We don't want to prioritize our own desires over the needs of others. Instead, we would prefer to follow the special calling God has given us: people who make a positive impact on the world, just like the mothers we have long admired.

So build a life centered around the values of motherhood—love, kindness, and selflessness. It won't always be easy—there may be long days, dirty diapers, loads of laundry, and muddy floors, but it is so exciting to see where the journey takes us. At the end of the day, those hard moments are lost in the big hugs, laughter, and tears we share with our children, making memories to last a lifetime.

And remember, the next time you see a younger mom with a buggy full of kids—grabbing her groceries and staring off into space, likely thinking about the million other things she needs to get done that day—stop and offer a smile or a word of encouragement. We have all been there and the last thing we need is to give into the world's ideas. It would be better to stand on God's side with this one.

There is so much joy in being a mother and getting to experience all the love that comes from it

Protect Them

Train up a child in the way he should go: and
when he is old, he will not depart from it.

—Proverbs 22:6

As new parents, you spend so much time researching
and trying to learn all the things that are helpful or
beneficial to your children. There are long days and
sleepless nights. There are moments when you feel as
though you are failing in every way, especially when
things just don't seem to be going the way the latest
self-help book tells you they should.

Don't give up! Keep up the good work! While
searching for all the information to help you parent,
don't forget that God gave us all the tools we needed
to prepare our children for life and raise them to
make better choices. It all starts at home with the
family. As parents, we are commanded to take the

time and train, teach and show our children the way of Christ.

> Children are a gift from the
> Lord; they are a reward from him.
> (Psalm 127:3)

The world would tell us that children are just an option or a burden. They are so much more. The Bible clearly states that children are gifts. What we do with that gift is up to us. I have failed many times in making sure that I remember what kind of gift they are. We see cute little faces and sweet smiles. However, as cute as they may be, they are our responsibility to teach, correct, and protect.

We have to set aside our own selfish desires for the easy way out and take time to truly invest in our children to stay involved and to be always aware of everything that is going on that they could be affected or influenced by.

When we keep asking why our world is going in the direction it is, it is clearly because man has taken everything that God has taught us and tried to change it and corrupted it to fit their own sinful, selfish desires. If we as parents don't take a stand and fight back, it will only get worse.

Stop buying the products, stop going to the theme parks, and stop letting a cell phone act as a pacifier for your children. Stop investing in things that undermine everything we as parents desire and labor to pour into and mold our children toward.

If we lock our doors to keep evil people out of our homes, why would we purchase potentially harmful things for our children, bring them into our homes, or take them places that adhere to a known agenda and not expect consequences?

To some, that may seem harsh, but let it be. Rather than be upset with me, be upset with those who see fit to hurt your children mentally, spiritually, and even physically.

Protect your children from all that you can and prepare them for the moments when you aren't there. Help them understand and be confident in their beliefs. Remind them to completely put their faith and trust in God.

Fathers, lead, guide, and protect your children. Mothers, love, nurture, and teach your children. When we do this in our homes, we won't have to worry as much about what the world is throwing at us. Our children will be prepared to fight back alongside us. This is when the culture changes.

The Beauty of Patriarchy in the Home

A husband and father is the head of his household, a family leader, provider, and protector. This is what patriarchy really looks like. The world would tell us differently, but scripture soundly begs to differ. It's baffling to look it up and see there is now a definition as it would relate to a world of feminism.

As a young married woman, I had never even heard the word patriarchy and had no idea that what I had been shown growing up was just that. I grew up thinking that I would meet the man of my dreams on some big white horse, and he would whisk me away to a beautiful forever, and life would be wonderful and easy.

We were both young when we married and in love and thought we knew exactly what we were doing. We definitely gave it our all for a good long time. I then began to realize that if things didn't go just the way I wanted them to, I would smile and bat my eyes, and my loving husband would give in to avoid the confrontation that would follow. I am terribly ashamed that I behaved that way.

Of course, we both made many mistakes, and we have learned a lot over the years of being together. To be honest, it wasn't until we were under strong shepherding by our pastor that things really began to change. My heart began to really understand the scripture and what God meant by submission.

I thought back to the times of watching my mom and grandmothers cook and prepare the dinner table for the family and the many stories shared. It was always the ladies that sat down last, but not because they had to. It was because they wanted to. I strongly believe that it brings complete joy as a wife and mother to serve your family.

I think, like most women today, when you hear that word, you automatically think of control, or as the feminist would say, *domination*. That is a common misunderstanding. I say it's a misunderstanding, but it seems to only be that way in the marriage setting. It seems to be totally acceptable when it comes to our government but heavily resisted when it is commanded in our homes.

The beauty of completely relying on the man that God strategically places in your life is actually such a peaceful feeling. It's almost like it was designed that way. The simplicity it creates in life allows for such joy and relief from any undue pressure—the weight of leading, providing, and protecting falls on his shoulders.

We, as wives, have a wonderful opportunity to joyfully submit to our husbands who have submitted to Christ and walk daily beside them. This makes for a love story straight from scripture, not some silly romance novel. That, my friend, is the beauty of patriarchy in the home.

The Joy of Being a Grandparent

I honestly don't think anyone can prepare you for the overwhelming joy that comes with being a grandparent. In the months leading up to their birth, you begin to want to purchase everything you see that is baby related, and the minute they are born, something in you changes.

I can't put into words what the feeling is like, but if you have experienced it, you would likely understand. I remember asking my mom several times before my grandson was born what it was like. She could never put it into words either. She could only say that I would understand as soon as he gets here.

It is such a blessing that we are given the opportunity to raise our children and then that God graciously allows us to see our children grow and raise children of their own. While I can't explain the feeling of the joy it brings, I can tell you that the feeling of responsibility changed for me.

I started to look back over my life. I began questioning if I took enough time to make sure that my children knew they were loved. I don't mean loved by buying all the latest gadgets or name-brand clothes, I mean actually sitting and spending time with them and teaching them about life. More importantly, did I show Christ daily? After asking myself those questions, the answers were ones that I didn't really enjoy hearing.

Of course, nobody's perfect. We all make mistakes and God's grace is sufficient to cover a multitude of sins, however, I wanted to learn from my past mistakes and take more time not only with my children but also invest in the additional little blessing that made me a *Gigi*. I wanted to be more intentional with my time, thoughts, and actions.

I think sometimes life can get so distracting that we lose sight of some of the most important moments in our lives. Buying a house was great, but I miss the sound of the little footsteps running through the halls more than the home. Buying a car was fun, but I miss cleaning up the crumbs in the backseat. Signing up for football was a blast, but I miss him asking me to tie his shoes. Going to pick out the pretty leotard for dance was lovely, but watching my little girl twirl around in front of the mirror is a moment I will never forget.

Having a grandson, I feel like I get a second chance. I get a chance to slow down completely and watch every little detail. I got to be there when he held his little head up on his own. I was there when he rolled over for the first time and when he giggled so sweetly. I light up inside every time he reaches out his little arms for me to pick him up and our afternoon wagon rides are the best.

So maybe I can explain the feeling a bit better now. I think it's honestly pure joy! A joy that God has chosen to share with us to remind us that we all get a second chance. What a joy it is to be a grandparent.

Kindness Still Exists

In a world full of confusion and uncertainty, taking the time to show a little extra kindness and compassion is never a bad idea.

I was constantly reminded as a child growing up that treating others the way you would want to be treated was so important. Did I get that right every day? No, I failed daily. We are human; we are not perfect. Though we aren't perfect, using that as an excuse shouldn't be an opportunity to not show kindness.

There have been many times over the past couple of years that I have thought there was no hope and that most had forgotten what true kindness and compassion looked like. Yesterday, my hope was restored.

While waiting my turn at my doctor's office, I watched as an elderly man was pushed in his wheelchair by a younger gentleman who looked to be in his midtwenties. They were talking and laughing a bit. I watched them very closely because the young man seemed so respectful and helpful to not only the gentleman but everyone else as well.

He constantly watched to see if anyone needed the door opened for them to go out, and if they did, he rushed over to make sure he was there to do it. At one point, the elderly gentleman was concerned about his hair, and I watched as the young man fixed it for him and reminded him how handsome he was.

I honestly had to hold back the tears. They weren't family, so this was not expected of the young man. Obviously, this young man's parents did an amazing job of teaching him how important showing kindness and genuine respect really is.

This young man had no idea that anyone was watching. He wasn't doing it for that. It was apparent that his care and compassion were true and genuine. I don't know if anyone else saw it or if it affected them the way it did me, but my day truly brightened.

It was a beautiful reminder that taking the time to show kindness hasn't been forgotten. We should all be reminded that one day someone may be pushing us in our wheelchair to our next appointment, and I don't know about you, but I definitely want to be treated the way this gentleman was treated.

So today, take that extra moment to smile at someone, hold a door, pay a compliment, give a hug, or just remind someone that you are there to help if they need it. Pay it forward! Let this young man inspire you as he did me. Remind the world that kindness still exists and it really does matter.

Expectations

I find my life is a lot easier the lower
I keep my expectations.

—Bill Watterson

I have learned over the years through many different experiences, that we set expectations for life, for others, and for ourselves so high that they become unattainable. We forget that we are all human. We have families, work, responsibilities and so much more.

Even when we know that we are so busy, we continue to expect others around us to have the time that we can't seem to find ourselves.

A very wise friend shared with me that when we lower those expectations and begin to show grace to those around us that we would want to be shown to us, time begins to be so much more enjoyable.

This does not mean that we just accept bad treatment from others, it just means that when people make mistakes like we all will do that you offer an olive branch, a bit of grace, and forgiveness.

Maybe it's a missed call or a long-forgotten text message. I am certainly guilty when it comes to this but not intentionally. Life happens. The dishes need washing, the eggs need to be gathered, and my laundry needs to be folded. In my head, like most, I saw it and responded. Then the day kept moving and the chores got done.

When we set expectations for people that we will never meet, it only causes disappointment.

As I have gotten older, the truest friendships have been the ones that understand that biblically we are called to care for our homes first. Our relationship with Christ, our spouse, and our children should be at the top of our list. When your circle of friends lives these things out, they understand.

I think the advice my dear friend shared with me took not only the pressure off myself and allowed me to not overcommit, but it also made me take pressure off others. I learned that only God can meet all of my needs and he is the only one I should turn to for that. The friendships that we are blessed with along the way are just the cherry on top.

Life is short and most days it is hard. We are all either in a storm or coming out of a storm. Grant a bit more grace today. Grant it to yourself and others. Find joy in the little things and when the big things happen, celebrate. Never let the little disappointments ruin your day!

It's Okay to Say No

I've always struggled with being a people-pleaser.

I was the one who felt as if I would be letting someone down if I didn't say yes to help with everything, so I would constantly agree to every request, no matter how it might inconvenience or overwhelm me. I honestly felt as though it would be impolite to say no, and I didn't want to disappoint anyone.

This mentality grew increasingly stressful for me and my family. I was constantly drained, anxious, and unable to cope with everything I had added to my plate.

Enough was enough. After some wonderful Christian counseling, I realized that it was okay to say no. I needed to set boundaries for my mental health. I needed to prioritize my time with my husband and children.

Over time, I began to identify the activities and people draining my energy and causing me stress. I also sat down and made a list of the things that were important to me. When someone would ask me to do something, I would pause and consider whether it aligned with my priorities. If it didn't, I began to say no, politely but firmly. And in saying no, I was actually saying yes to myself and my well-being.

At first, I of course worried that my friends and family would be disappointed or upset with me for saying no. But to my surprise, they were very understanding and even more supportive of the new boundaries.

As I started saying no more often, I found more time and energy for the things that were important to fulfilling my role as a wife and mother. I had more time to focus on hobbies—mainly those outside with the farm and my chickens—which left me feeling much happier and more fulfilled. My mental health also improved as I spent more time equipping my faith through Scripture, reading to manage my stress and anxiety.

By setting boundaries and prioritizing your spiritual and mental health, along with important family time, you, too, will be able to live a more balanced and fulfilling life. It's important to remember that God calls us to do some things, but not all things. When we are focused on fulfilling our purpose in his will, things are much easier to accomplish. It is only when we start adding extra plans that everything gets overwhelming.

Friends, some days are harder than others and the only thing you can do is the next thing, and that is it. You will certainly have many things to keep you going, but it is okay to say no when there just isn't extra time. Our families need us as much as we need them. Keep your head up, and don't feel the need to apologize for fulfilling the tasks God has given you first. If there is time after that, lend a hand when you are able.

Misery Loves Company, Don't Request an Invite

Have you stopped to look at the people you pass in your local grocery store, convenience store, or super-market lately? I have started doing just that, making it a point to smile at each and every one that I pass along the way.

I receive very few smiles in return. It's not just a specific age of people. I pass all ages and they all look as if they might break something were they to smile back at me.

I often wonder: Is there something on my face? Maybe there's something in my teeth, or maybe my hair is sticking straight up and I don't realize it?

It has to be something, right? I mean, who doesn't love to smile?

"Why do so many people look so unhappy?" I asked myself. Is it the masks? Perhaps we wore those stupid things for so long that we have forgotten that we can smile. And what were those masks really hiding? Most of us know that they weren't preventing a virus. What they seem to have messed with is our ability to show joy!

Our world seems to be filled with more stress and anxiety. Constant restlessness and impatience for things to happen will steal your joy and rob you of precious time and priceless moments. As one of my favorite authors, Elisabeth Elliot, wrote, "Restlessness and impatience change nothing except our peace and joy." Our joy doesn't come from ourselves, other people, or material things, it comes from God.

According to Elliot, "The world looks for happiness through self-assertion. The Christian knows that joy is found in self-abandonment. 'If a man will let himself be lost for My sake,' Jesus said, 'he will find his true self.'"

I know that there are most definitely moments in life when a smile is hard to find, but let that moment pass and remember that you have so much to be joyful about. You are breathing, you have life, and you have family or friends that love you. You are here for a purpose.

There are no accidents in this life, my friend, only God's will. He trusts us to be a light in a world of darkness and to share his love with others. Many times you will share your joy and feel that it goes unnoticed, but don't stop.

There are many who are struggling with things we are unaware of who may later remember your smile or your kind gesture. There are those who feel hopeless and may stop and think after seeing your smile, that they, too, have a reason to smile.

Continue to smile, and you might just get one back. It would be pretty awesome if everyone reading this did just that. Maybe then the table of misery wouldn't have so many guests seated at it, for the table of joy would be the new place to be.

Taking Time to Rejuvenate Your Marriage

My husband and I recently embarked on a little weekend getaway to relax and unwind. I was super excited and ready to go, as was he. Of course, not everything went according to plan!

We left late, nearly missing the most beautiful, breathtaking sunset I have ever seen.

Upon arriving at our cabin in the woods, we unpacked, then started a campfire outside. It felt like it was just us and the woods, peaceful…until we heard the not-so-peaceful music coming from the cabin above ours. We couldn't help but laugh about it, knowing that those campers were enjoying their time just as we were trying to enjoy ours.

The next day we headed out for a hike to explore the beautiful surroundings. Of course, it started to rain. Luckily, we were dressed well enough, so we made the best of things and tried to enjoy the hike for a short time. We did! The scenery was gorgeous, seemingly extending for miles. There were no emails to check, no messages to read, and no phone calls to be made. It was just the two of us walking together through winding trails, holding hands as we climbed difficult terrains.

We've been doing this throughout our marriage, it just looked and felt a little different at this moment. Maybe because it was so quiet and there was nothing else to focus on but us. I began thinking of all the things we overcame together, with God's wonderful grace and mercy, of course!

That grace extended to us even more that evening upon returning from dinner at a quaint little restaurant in town. My husband knew that we could encounter fog on the way back up the mountain, and we certainly did, for we could hardly see two to three feet in front of the car! I was internally panicking, but my husband was completely calm as we talked our way up that mountain, hugging the left side of the road to avoid driving off the edge. I completely trusted him with my life, and he calmed all my fears. We finally made it back to the cabin, and I think that was the happiest moment!

God was protecting us throughout our trip, just as he has our entire marriage.

I am not one to give marriage advice, for I have made every mistake in the book, but because of God, our marriage is a miracle and a wonderful testimony and blessing. God belongs at the center of your marriage, your family, and all that you do in life. If you get that right, you're a lot further along than most people.

In addition to placing God at the center of your marriage, it also helps to communicate openly and honestly with your spouse. Effective communication done respectfully and constructively is the foundation of any healthy relationship.

Spending quality time together, without distractions, is also crucial for strengthening the bond between partners. Couples should plan regular date nights or weekends away to reconnect and rejuvenate their relationship.

It's easy to take each other for granted in a long-term relationship, so remember to also show appreciation and gratitude toward your spouse.

Conflicts are a natural part of any relationship. But listening to each other's perspectives, finding common ground, and working toward a solution that works for you both are a few ways to resolve conflicts constructively.

Finally, practice forgiveness daily! No one is perfect, and mistakes are bound to happen in any relationship. Practicing forgiveness and letting go of past hurts helps any couple move forward in their relationship. Forgiveness does not mean forgetting the past, but rather acknowledging the hurt, learning from it, and moving on.

Overall, the key to a healthy and fulfilling marriage is to cultivate a strong foundation of faith, trust, respect, and love. My husband and I took our trip to do just that.

Imagine if every couple took the time to stop and see all the wonderful things and focus on those rather than the few bad things! How many homes would be unbroken and how many kids would understand better what true marriage looks like? It's not a fairy tale, my friends, it's the journey of a lifetime!

The Greatest of These Is Love

So now faith, hope, and love abide, these
three; but the greatest of these is love.
—1 Corinthians 13:13

I am sure that most of you have read the scriptures that eloquently explain to us what love should actually be. However, I myself have struggled with loving exactly the way we are commanded.

We see these words at most wedding ceremonies, and it seems so sweet and romantic, but do we really understand the meaning?

Love is patient and kind; love does not envy or boast; it is not arrogant or rude. It does not insist on its own way; it is not irritable or resentful; it does not rejoice at wrongdoing, but rejoices with the truth. Love bears all things, believes all things, hopes all things, endures all things.

On a daily basis just being consistently patient and kind can be hard for anyone. Then we are called to not be irritable or resentful, which means you should have a joyful attitude at all times. I don't know about you, but that isn't the easiest thing to do. Our flesh definitely fights against that.

We as humans are selfish beings, and until we completely submit to Christ, showing complete joy and love will be hard for us. The people of the world have made it their mission to show us a different way to love, which if you pay attention, has caused confusion and heartache. God is not the author of confusion which is comforting in itself.

Learning to completely trust in this and lean on it has given me such peace. When we trust in ourselves, we tend to let ourselves down. We are human. That doesn't mean we give up. God's awesome grace and mercy that is freely given to us daily is a reminder that we don't have to carry the burdens alone. He walks with us.

In marriage and in life, things get hard, but when we let go of doing it our way and totally surrender to Christ something amazing happens. The joy begins to flow and you learn to enjoy life. Even the little things bring you happiness. A big life full of material things and unwarranted expectations can be so draining, but a simple life filled with joy and love and fulfilling relationships makes for a much better life lived.

Remember that love is a big word and a big task, but we are told that God's love also covers a multitude of sins. I want to show that kind of love as well. I hope you will too.

We all could use a little more love, forgiveness, and joy in our lives. Remember when you're frustrated or irritated with someone else God chooses to love us even when we're unlovable.

The Rewards of Caregiving
for Elderly Parents

My husband and I recently began spending much more one-on-one time with his parents. Things look a bit different now as they have gotten older. Alzheimer's has a way of interrupting things and making life a little bit more difficult, so we're staying very close to make sure they have everything they need from cooking to cleaning to making sure things are taken care of on their property.

Our parents spend so much time raising us and pouring into our lives, and then the roles get reversed, and we are the ones taking care of them.

There are days that seem totally normal, and then there are those that leave you wondering if your loved ones are still in there. Each day brings both joy and sadness. Their confusion is mixed with simple things that light up their day and bring joy to them like that of a small child.

Caregiving for our parents can be somewhat overwhelming, but in the end more rewarding than anything, and I am quickly learning that these treasured moments with loved ones are undeniably the best thing that comes from caring for them in the later part of their lives.

No two days are the same. There are days that are uneventful and somewhat peaceful and there are days where confusion sets in, and you are left explaining things over and over in a cycle that you think will never end.

There are also moments of pure joy, where you don't know whether to laugh or cry. One of these happened this past Sunday. Those who know my father-in-law realize that he can be a bit grumpy, but generally a lovable old man. He was in a bit of a mood that day and continued to question something that he was having a hard time understanding. Then my mother-in-law began to sing "Amazing Grace." Within a few seconds, my father-in-law forgot about his concern and started singing along with her.

It was at that moment that everything calmed down, the confusion passed, and life felt absolutely normal again. I had to hide my tears with laughter.

Even though there are many tough moments, days, and even weeks, I wouldn't trade any of them for anything. The time that I get to spend with my amazing mother-in-law and father-in-law—the people who lovingly raised my husband—is a blessing to me.

I pray daily that my children feel the same way when my mind doesn't work as well as it used to, and I forget who they are. I pray that they will experience the same joy in taking care of their parents as we experienced in taking care of them as small children.

Our time here on earth is precious, but it just doesn't seem to last long enough, so it is such a blessing to be able to give back to the ones who have given so much to us. There are many friends and family members who have experienced these same moments and I know they wouldn't trade those for anything.

So even when the days are hard and the nights are long, share love and understanding—and patience too—remembering that someday, it might be you.

Thank You, Dad

I am sure most of you are familiar with Mike Rowe, host of the very popular show on Discovery Network, *Dirty Jobs*. I have watched his show and many times thought to myself that there is absolutely no amount of money in the world that would get me to do certain jobs he covered.

Most of us, if not all of us, have thought the same thing at one time or another. We realize things have to get done, and we just don't want to be the ones to do it. After reading his SWEAT Pledge, a small portion of which can be found below, it became clear to me the reason he chose to showcase those certain tasks. I also believe that my dad secretly helped write it.

Partial SWEAT Pledge as follows:

"The SWEAT Pledge" (Skill and Work Ethic Aren't Taboo)

I do not "follow my passion." I bring it with me. I believe that any job can be done with passion and enthusiasm.

I believe the best way to distinguish myself at work is to show up early, stay late, and cheerfully volunteer for every crappy task there is.

I believe the most annoying sounds in the world are whining and complaining. I will never make them. If I am unhappy with my work, I will either find a new job or find a way to be happy.

I believe that all people are created equal. I also believe that all people make choices. Some choose to be lazy.

Some choose to sleep in. I choose to work my butt off.

Growing up, I learned that if you don't work, you don't eat. To put it in nicer terms, having a good, strong work ethic was not an option in our home. Whether you were washing dishes or mowing the lawn, you did it with a good attitude and to the very best of your ability. That was shown daily to myself and my brother by our parents and grandparents. To this day, my dad is still the first to the office and a lot of times the last to leave.

I can remember getting so upset with my dad after cutting the grass because I enjoyed doing it most of the time. Something about making perfect lines in the yard was fun to me. However, he had eyes that never missed a thing, especially when it came to that one blade of grass that I missed in the front yard.

It would be a Friday afternoon, and I would be ready to go spend the night with one of my friends, and he would take me out to show me what I missed and what I needed to fix before I left the house. Boy, my blood would boil.

As I have gotten older, those moments have become so valuable to me. The standard he set caused me to raise the standards I set for myself. I realized that having a good work ethic and doing it with the right attitude will move you further along in life than the best bought-and-paid-for education most times.

I see that lacking so much in our young adults today. It is almost as if they expect the very best from the beginning in all things with a lack of enthusiasm and a strong work ethic to follow. We have forgotten the days of starting from the bottom and earning your way to the top. We need to remember that! It doesn't matter what job you have; people will pay attention to the way you do it.

I haven't taken the time to thank my dad enough for the good things he taught me, but I hope he sees that I was paying attention even though it didn't seem like it at the time. I pray that whatever God calls you to do, you will show up to do it with enthusiasm and encourage others to do the same.

You never know who is watching and where it will lead you. Thank you, Dad!

Thank You, Mom!

Her children rise up and call her blessed; her husband also, and he praises her: "Many women have done excellently, but you surpass them all."
—Proverbs 31:28–29

I have been blessed with the best mom who has impacted my life in countless ways.

A significant influence in my life, my mom has shaped me into the woman I have become. From the countless hours she spent showing and teaching me things, to the emotional support she has offered throughout my life, she has become my closest and most cherished friend.

One of her greatest qualities is her unconditional love. Mom always loves me, regardless of what I have done or what mistakes I make. In loving me, she also provides great wisdom and advice, pointing me to God, the only answer to all of life's problems.

She shares her faith not only through her words but also most importantly through her actions.

Her silence and strong faith during some of life's hardest trials likely taught me more than anything else. Her ability to stay strong and take care of her family during these moments was something I never understood…until I became a mom myself.

Patience is another great quality she never lacked. She taught me to be patient and kind to others and to treat them the way I would want to be treated. Learning to show this kind of patience to others usually blessed me so much more than it did the other person.

As I grew older, she spent many hours teaching me important values, such as being a blessing as a wife and being a good friend and a loving mom. She taught me that honesty and compassion go hand in hand. She led by example, and those values will stay with me for the rest of my life.

From the time we are born, moms hold us and console us, they redirect our attitudes as tantrum-throwing toddlers, and for us girls, they patiently handle our many emotional moments, reminding us that we shouldn't let those emotions overcome us. My mom is still here to offer guidance and support, helping me navigate the challenges of adult life with grace and courage.

Whether I need a shoulder to cry on, someone to share my successes with, or just someone to be a listening ear, she is always there.

My mom is also incredibly hardworking. She seemed to always sacrifice her own needs and desires to ensure that we, her children, had everything we needed. There were many hours spent staying up all night to care for a sick child, many nights of cooking, piles of laundry that had to be done, messes that needed cleaning, and the list goes on.

I never heard her complain once about any of it. She just kept giving when it didn't seem like she should have anything left to give. She is still that way today, and if you know her, you are blessed. She is a phenomenal lady, a picture of grace, and if you asked her, it has everything to do with Christ.

Just as I was influenced by her, so she was influenced by her mom and other ladies in her life. I pray that she knows how much that influence passed down has meant to me, and I also pray that the same will be said of me by my children.

We, mothers, have tough jobs, but they are the most rewarding. God has entrusted us with a big task, but He gives much guidance through scripture and the ladies He strategically places in our lives along the way.

Celebrate your mom every day, not just this day!

Memories Are Moments You Carry with You for a Lifetime

I recently talked with a friend who is going through some of the same things that my husband and I went through when we decided to buy an old historic home.

Located in the beautiful downtown area of our city, I first saw our home when my husband actually sent me to look at the house for sale next door. I just knew I saw a diamond in the rough in the neighboring house, though, and had to have it. I thought we could take this house and make it our home.

Most people thought we were absolutely crazy, for the house needed so much work. You literally could see the ground through the hardwood floor in one of the bedrooms. It's funny now to think about, but it wasn't then.

After many discussions with our family—many of which found them looking at us as if we had lost our minds—we put an offer on the rundown house and it was accepted. The house was worth absolutely nothing, so we had to gut the whole thing and start from scratch.

It took us at least ten months to complete the renovations. We lived with my husband's parents and found ourselves juggling small children, our jobs, and late-night work in the house. You can imagine the stress that put on our family. Looking back, there were so many laughs we should have had, but at the time, there were tears and lots of frustration. In this frustration, there were also beautiful memories made.

I will never forget when we finally moved in, walking our kids to the local elementary school as my daughter started kindergarten and my son began first grade. In this home, we had birthday parties, we celebrated Christmas and Thanksgiving, we hosted family get-togethers, and we had many late nights in the kitchen with our teenaged kids and their friends. We hosted exchange students. We brought animals home, making them a part of the family until it was their time to go, and then burying them in the backyard.

As time went on, my children got older, and my son went off to college. Then a wonderful young man came along and asked to marry my daughter, so just my husband and I were left, and there was way too much house for just the two of us. We knew it was time to sell, but we had no idea what we were going to move on to.

I remember packing up boxes and packing up memories, looking at the different imperfections on the wall where one kid had colored with a pencil and another scratched something, or where the dog got ahold of the baseboard. These slight imperfections in our home brought back so many beautiful memories and I wanted to take everyone with me, knowing we were about to close on the house and have our last night there.

I also remember the looks on my kids' faces, the sadness that this house where so many things happened would not be our home anymore.

But once the move finally happened and we were away, we all realized that it was not the house that made the home, it was us. It was our family. It was the moments we shared together, it was the things we did together. Those memories were ours and we could carry them with us wherever we went.

Occasionally we drive by the old house just to see how it's changed. The paint is different, as are the decorations. It doesn't look like our house anymore because it isn't. We miss our home, but now we're making new memories.

If you are going through something like this—building a home, looking for one, or even remodeling it—remember that it's not about the structure itself, it's about the people who are in it. Cherish those people, cherish those moments, and take your memories with you wherever you go.

Living the Dream and Homesteading

Growing up, I spent almost every summer working with my grandparents on their farm. Most of this was fun to me as a child. We were either planting or harvesting. Even shelling the peas—which took hours to do—was fun simply because it provided time to sit on the front porch and talk with my grandparents.

As I got older, my grandmother passed away and the farm was no more. I honestly never thought farming would be something that I would get to do anymore.

But that changed in the last two years. My husband and I became empty nesters. I had big dreams of traveling, but with the rising cost of living and gas prices, my dreams dwindled fast. Instead, we decided to sell our house and almost everything we owned and move out to the family property.

Suddenly, the things I learned growing up on the farm began benefiting our family. My husband learned the same skills from his parents and grandparents and we began to put them to use. My wonderful husband, the dedicated planner, worked with me—the dreamer—to plant our first crop, and we soon discovered that everything you plant doesn't grow just the way you would like. Though disappointed at first, I began to realize that homesteading is a learning experience that teaches new lessons every day.

But planting and harvesting a crop wasn't the only thing I wanted to learn. I wanted chickens! My husband slowly came around to the idea, and before you knew it, we had fifteen.

With a lot of blood, sweat, and tears my husband built a chicken coop, and we began patiently waiting for the first egg to be laid. After what seemed like forever, one came, and when it did, you would have thought we won the lottery!

Today, I think we did. The cost of food is constantly rising and the price of eggs seems to be completely out of control. In the beginning, homesteading seemed like such a crazy leap of faith, but now it's turning into the greatest blessing.

For starters, the joy of being outside has allowed for a more simple, slow-paced life. From the first rooster crow and beautiful sunrise to the sky filled with colors unimaginable at sunset, I have more time to relax and enjoy all the many blessings of God's beautiful handiwork.

My homesteading adventure has also provided time to learn how important it is to be more self-sufficient. I now have peace of mind knowing that I am able to do just that.

We have eleven little ladies who are graciously producing four to six eggs per day, so collecting those and sharing them is another great joy. It has also been a great way of saving money. Those little nuggets of gold provide a great source of nutrition for us, my children, and my grandchild.

I honestly don't see things changing much as far as the cost of food. I tend to agree that the constant increase in egg prices is unwarranted and that some are piggybacking on the increase in our local grocery stores. For that reason, I recommend beginning your own little farm. We started homesteading to better our family, and the ever-rising costs are making that decision pay off. It's one small way we can stop being so dependent on the government.

I Regret That My Family Didn't Homeschool Earlier

Those who know my family know that we were always very supportive of our children's school activities while they were in the public school system. We were on boards, volunteered for multiple events—you name it, we did it.

But things changed around the time my children entered high school. My husband and I noticed a decline in what our children were learning. Labeled an athlete, my son became just a number in the classroom, requiring only the bare minimum of instruction to keep him on the playing field. And while my daughter didn't need as much one-on-one instruction as my son, she did need teachers to keep an eye on her when surrounded by boys who couldn't seem to behave in a respectful way toward young ladies.

We were also disturbed that the values and ethics we were trying to teach our children at home were not what they were learning at school. It felt like a war. Both my husband and I strongly believed that education was very important, but to put it bluntly, simply sending our children home with worksheets and hours of homework didn't seem like teaching to us.

After much prayer and discussion, our family decided to take our children out of the public school system and homeschool them. The decision was not made lightly. My son was a sophomore and very involved in sports, while my daughter was a freshman and involved in dance and many other school-related activities. Taking them out of public school seemed like it would disrupt these parts of life.

Our fears were needless. We joined an excellent cover school that walked us through all the details of educating our children. My children got involved, and it seemed as though they were meant to be there all along. My son began playing football and baseball competitively, eventually winning a college baseball scholarship, while my daughter played softball and volleyball and absolutely loved doing so.

But one of the best things about homeschooling was the overwhelming peace that leaving the public school system brought. The constant battle we experienced there became too much. Our home became a family of like-minded parents and children putting God first.

The peace I felt when we made the change also came with regret. I wished that we would have made the decision to homeschool sooner! But I comfort myself that we didn't have the knowledge and understanding at that time that we do now, and God worked things out exactly as He planned. We are forever grateful for the journey.

I tell my story because there are many parents currently struggling with their children's school systems. Making the decision to homeschool is hard, especially for working parents, but it's important to realize that even while there are great teachers out there when the government gets involved in education, all the good ideas go out the window. Sadly, the old way of teaching is a thing of the past, replaced with a cookie-cutter system filled with endless days of training robots.

Our children deserve better! It may take some sacrifice, but giving your child the best education and the best environment to learn in is so important and provides a great return on investment.

College is one example. Many college admission offices actively seek homeschoolers, and studies show that coming from a homeschool background helps students graduate at a higher rate than those from a traditional education background. Another example is the opportunity to teach your children to think outside of the box, a quality that will help them succeed in life. And most importantly, homeschooling gives parents the opportunity to teach their children about Christ every day.

Leaving a Legacy That Won't Be Forgotten

We recently celebrated my grandson's first birthday. It reminded me how fast time passes by and the precious nature of each and every moment. The moments that I spent with my grandparents as a young child made such an impact on my life, and I would love for my grandson to treasure our memories just as much, so I have tried my best to soak up as much time with him as possible.

Becoming a grandparent is one of the most wonderful feelings in the world. Compared with raising my own children, it's so much easier to spoil grandchildren! It is all too easy to give into the constant urge to treat them to something special.

As a grandparent, I am learning that the greatest legacy I can leave my grandchildren is the memories we create together. I would love for my grandchildren to remember me not just for the gifts I give them, but for the time they spent with me and the love we share.

Those little deposits of time—teaching them and enjoying life with them—are true gifts worth far more than any money can buy, even though they don't come wrapped in a shiny package with a big bow. These things are a true inheritance that will benefit their lives even after you are gone.

Sharing your faith and stories of God's continued faithfulness in your family is one aspect of this inheritance. I pray that my grandchildren will grow to trust God's faithfulness in their own life by seeing and hearing about it firsthand from both their parents and grandparents.

Another aspect of this inheritance is the tiny moments you spend with them. This may be a simple wagon ride, or the planting of a garden and playing in the dirt. Perhaps it's watching Papa build a chicken coop or process a deer. Maybe it's feeding the chickens, feeling a farm fresh egg, or learning why eating rocks isn't a good idea—even though they look so fun to try!

This inheritance may also just mean quiet time on the farm, sitting with the roosters as they work the summer garden land, being alarmed every time they make a loud crow to remind you they are there. It's also the giggles that come from the licks to the face of the family pet, or the lit-up face when daddy gets the four-wheeler out to go for a ride, or momma runs to tickle him.

Your moments may look different, but they are just that…your moments, and they are so important and precious. You can leave a large monetary inheritance to your grandchildren, but it is these little moments that will have an even bigger impact on their lives and their own children's lives.

Finally, when working to leave this inheritance, it is also important to remember that we are the grandparents, not the parents, and respect for their rules and boundaries is very important. Discussing these is crucial to warding off any hard feelings. Most of the time, your children will be very appreciative of your willingness to invest in your grandchildren, leaving a legacy of love and memories rather than a stack of toys that one day will find their place in the donation box.

Leave an inheritance, leave a legacy! Let it be one of love and a lifetime of memories that won't be forgotten.

God Will Carry You through the Storm

This article contains one of the hardest things I have ever shared with my readers. Despite the difficulty, it is part of my story, and I believe it is important for others to know that all the happy stories we read don't come without tough times. I am human just like you, so life hits me hard at different times just like it does for millions of others. God has truly blessed me and sharing that with others is important.

In 2016, our family faced a difficult time. It was a situation that none of us ever expected, and like others, we certainly never expected it to happen to us, but it did, and I had honestly never experienced trauma like it before. In the end, the amount of stress and anxiety it caused was almost too much for me to bear.

As a wife and mother of two, I felt like I was strong enough to handle anything. I was wrong. I could not sleep. I could not function. It was such a gut-wrenching experience that I had trouble putting one foot in front of the other. Thus, I entered a time of coping, for that was all I knew to do.

After weeks of anxiety and many unknowns, I turned to my physician for help rather than my pastor. I know that in some instances we need both, but my situation proved otherwise.

I remember making my appointment and sitting to talk to my doctor. I really just needed help to make sense of the chaos surrounding me and the unanswered questions I had. But my doctor felt that giving me medication to fix each one of those issues would be my best solution, so I trusted him.

At first, the medication helped. I began to rest better, and my anxiety began to calm down somewhat. But my family's ordeal lasted for over three years, so after a while, the medication didn't work as well, and I fell into a very dark place.

As hard as it was for me to endure this, it was even harder for my family to watch me allow stress, anxiety, and the need to medicate to overcome my life. It is hard even to share this with anyone, but

I believe there are others out there that have gone through or are going through a similar situation.

Physicians aren't God and never will be! They aren't all bad, but your research must be done before jumping into any treatment.

I do believe that allowing our minds to wander off too far can cause us to drift into a state of depression, and if not recognized early, the outcomes aren't good for anyone. So rather than stigmatize others or shun them over mental health problems, love them. Recognize the signs.

I became so good at hiding what was really going on, that only those closest to me could see what was happening. I could have destroyed so much, just because I felt like there was no hope.

I am very fortunate to have a wonderful husband, children, pastor, and church family that came around to love me during what felt like the darkest days of my life. They didn't provide magic pills, but they gave me sound, biblical counsel, and accountability, walking through the battle with me. They enabled me to not feel guilty and also to know that I was not alone. That love was hard at times, but it was what I needed.

I am now blessed with the best physician who knows my story and won't allow me to get back to that dark place.

My outlook has also changed. I removed myself from things that triggered me and made better decisions. I have learned to say no. My circle isn't as big as it once was and that's okay. Instead, I am focused on fulfilling the purpose God has for me in bringing glory to Him as a wife, mother, grandmother, daughter, caretaker, homemaker, and friend. I am blessed to have a job that allows me to work from home and share little parts of my life with others.

I pray that this story blesses others who also struggle and that in sharing this, they, too, will learn that there is hope. God will carry you through the storm and the joy on the other side is indescribable. Trust Him!

A Day of Thanksgiving

Time with family is priceless. The moments we spend together creating memories are ones that will never be forgotten.

As a young girl, I can remember my family preparing for the Thanksgiving meal and what each person would bring. I remember the laughs, the smell of sweet potato pie, and the occasional pop on the hand for trying to sneak food before it was time to eat.

The sound of all the children running around, going in and out of the house and smiling the biggest smiles. The strong aroma of Memaw's famous chicken and dumplings, and the overwhelming feeling of love comforted each and every person that walked through the door.

For our family, music was such a central part of every family gathering. You didn't have to wonder if we were going to sit around and sing and play instruments, you knew we were. We would sing old hymns and listen as my Poppy, and others would play every instrument you could think of. We never wanted to leave, and there didn't seem to be enough time to do it all in one day.

As we have all gotten older and some have gone on to be with our heavenly father, our lives seem to have gotten busier and we haven't been able to be together as much as we used to. The children have grown up, gotten married, some have moved away, and all have had children of their own.

This year will be different, almost all of us will be together again. We will plan the big meal and all the ladies will work together to prepare all the fixings, while the men cook the meat. We will sit at the table together and thank God for his many blessings on our family and then we will worship together singing hymns. I can't wait!

When you're young, you think life will last forever. You think your parents and grandparents are indestructible. You catch moments like butterflies and then let them fly away, thinking they will always return.

Then you grow up and you realize that life is short. You realize that all the extra stuff we add to our day doesn't really matter. You start to wish you could go back to the days of sitting for hours and laughing together as a family. You start to wish that every day was like Thanksgiving Day.

We are not promised the next second of our lives. I challenge you as I challenge myself: Put down the phone, hug your family tight, and take time to enjoy the smallest of things. Be silly, play outside with the kids, sing another song, share another story, and listen to all of the advice from your grandparents.

God has blessed us with so many wonderful things, and He gives us blessings even in the midst of the hardest trials we face. Start each day with a heart of gratitude! Make every day a day of Thanksgiving!

Christmas Traditions

With the Christmas season upon us, many are trying to find the perfect gift for everyone on their lists. I myself have been in the very same situation. I stopped recently and thought about all the things I got as a child and honestly can't remember many of the gifts.

I could really only ponder on the moments, the laughs, the funny Christmas pajamas and how my mom always wanted to take pictures the minute we woke up without brushing our hair or our teeth. And my mom ever so patiently waited until the day after Thanksgiving to put the tree up and all of the colorful decorations. The Christmas music would start playing, and there would be a different feeling in the air. Plans were made, menus were discussed and lists were given.

As we get older, the lists really never seemed to matter as much as we thought. I could have done without all the cool new toys and just enjoyed cooking with my mom and my memaw and listening to her sing. Maybe could have taken a little extra time to learn to play the guitar like my dad or an extra few minutes to help with the last-minute touches to the decorations around the house.

I don't know about you, but as I have gotten older, the material things just don't matter. The things you can't wrap and can't hold in your hands are the very things you wish you had more of. The moments in time that you can't get back are priceless!

My mom has always been the most generous person I know. She would literally give you the shirt off her back if you needed it. She works tirelessly every year preparing for the family to come and hardly sits down to enjoy it. Over the years, I have tried to make a point to go over before everyone else and spend a little extra time with her in the kitchen.

She doesn't know it, but those moments have been some of the best gifts to me. As children, we don't realize that the latest toys and gadgets will always be available, and there will always be new ones. However, our parents, grandparents, and other relatives will not always be around and the valuable lessons that they teach us and the family history that we learn from them will one day be forgotten if we don't take the time to soak it all in.

Christmas Eve, as long as I have been alive, my dad has sat with us and read the true story of Christmas from the Bible. The true meaning of Christmas is beautifully displayed in a story of love and simple means along with the birth of our Lord and Savior.

Every year, it seems that it is forgotten more and more, and we spend all of our time focusing on things that can be bought and returned rather than on things that can be cherished for many years to come. Imagine how long it took to string popcorn for tree trimmings, but I am sure the conversations included laughter and lots of love. It wasn't about spending money. It was about spending time with each other.

I pray that this year, during this Christmas season, you and I both will remember what's really important, the true reason for the season, and spend more time making traditions that last for the ages and less on the latest gadgets that will be forgotten.

A Christmas Tree Wish

This past week, my family and I took a short trip to the mountains. While we were there, we visited a few stores and did some shopping. I was taken aback by the small tree filled with hand-written wishes as I entered one of the stores.

There were so many written wishes. I wanted to stop and pray for each one. Most brought tears to my eyes, and then some a smile to my face and warmth in my heart.

I began to think about the people who wrote these. I wondered if they had prayed or knew the power of prayer. I wondered if anyone who saw them had stopped to pray for them as well.

With this tree, you only saw the wish, not who wrote it or any way to contact them or get them what they wished for. It was obvious that whoever passed by and took the time to read them would know that prayer was the only answer for each hand-written wish.

The more I read, the more my eyes filled with tears. Some wished for family members to beat cancer, to have peace in their homes, to have a fruitful marriage, to be able to be with their family at Christmas, and then others wished for a dog and snow and a *ring*!

I wondered what if someone gave me a card to write my wish on, what it would be. What would be the one thing I would like to wish for? There was just one thought that came to mind.

I'd wish that each and every person would know and feel the love of Christ. That has been the only thing to get me through all of the trials that I have faced in my life. It has also been the one and only thing that has been constant.

There are so many hurting and confused and feel as though no one is listening, but that is not true. God hears our thoughts and our prayers. He knows each and every concern we have. The answer may not always be what we expect it to be, but it is always in his perfect plan.

As I prayed for the wishes I read, I also prayed that even if the answer wasn't what they wanted that

God would wrap his loving arms around each one of them and that they would feel love like never before.

I pray the same things for you that are reading this. I pray that not only at Christmas but also all throughout the year. If you know someone who is struggling, pray for them too.

The world could definitely use a few more prayers and people reading the wishes on the trees. We all, though in different walks or times in our lives, could use a few extra prayers.

God bless you all, and Merry Christmas.

A New Year Centered around Christ and Not Ourselves

I don't know about you, but this past year has been full of ups and downs, good days and some not-so-good days, and many changes.

Actually, after I sit at the end of each year past, I think the same thing.

Even in the midst of all the uncertainty and inconveniences we face, we know God is with us. We know that His plan is perfect, and there is a reason for everything. If we go into this next year knowing and trusting in that, how much of a difference would that make for you and everyone around you?

There will always be something. A flat tire, an unexpected bill, a broken washer right before a big trip, a big decision to make that isn't easy. Trying to decide what to cut to make your family budget work better, or maybe it's taking care of a sick family member or even the unexpected loss of a friend or family member.

What if we chose joy rather than waiting for joy to find us even in the midst of these times in our lives? If we look at every situation as an opportunity rather than something to be fixed? We may not have enough money to go out to dinner, but how can we glorify God even more by staying home and sitting around a table to eat and fellowship with our loved ones?

You may have a flat tire, but rather than getting upset, take the time you have while you're waiting to see how many people cross your path whom you can share the joy of Christ with that wouldn't have been there if you hadn't gotten a flat tire.

This isn't easy for any of us to see while we are in the middle of the trial, including me. I am learning a little more as I get older to stop and realize that sometimes the trials are there to strengthen our testimony or to make us stop and be still and to see and appreciate the things and people around us.

When we continue to move at such a high speed in life, and everything seems to be going well, we forget how we got there and who really should be getting the glory. We as humans work hard and feel the need to do and take care of everything. Sometimes

God takes a moment to remind us that we are not in complete control and that He is and is always there with us.

I pray, with this new year, that we all take time to find joy even in the midst of the most trying times or aggravating circumstances.

Slow down and enjoy even the smallest of details. Take the photo and save the memory. Laugh a bit longer and remember what it feels like.

Spend a little longer with your family. Pray more, spend more time in worship, center this year around Christ rather than yourself or others, and see if this year is a little bit better than the last.

The Greatest Story
of Love Ever Told

Easter is often called the greatest love story ever told and for a very good reason. At its core, Easter is a story of love, sacrifice, and redemption that has captivated hearts and minds for centuries.

This beautiful story of sacrificial love begins with Jesus, God who became man, coming to earth to spread a message of love and compassion. He traveled far and wide, preaching to all who would listen about the importance of repenting, loving one another, caring for the less fortunate, and living a life of faith and service to others.

Despite his good deeds, Jesus was betrayed by one of his closest followers, arrested, and sentenced to death. He was beaten, mocked, and forced to carry his own cross up a hill called Golgotha. He was nailed to a cross and left to die, surrounded by those who had come to see him suffer.

Even as he hung dying on the cross, Jesus forgave His executioners and prayed for their salvation. He died so that all of humanity could be forgiven for their sins and find redemption. As the prophet Isaiah predicted hundreds of years before, "He was pierced for our transgressions; he was crushed for our iniquities; upon him was the chastisement that brought us peace, and with his wounds, we are healed."

Three days after his death, something incredible happened. Jesus rose from the dead, proving once and for all that love is stronger than death, and that the power of God's love can conquer even the darkest of evils.

This act of love and sacrifice is what makes Easter such a powerful and moving story. It reminds us that love can triumph over hate, that forgiveness can conquer sin, and that the greatest act of love is to lay down one's life for another.

As we celebrate Easter each year, we are reminded of this great love story, and we are called to love one another as Jesus loved us. We are called to forgive those who have wronged us, to care for the less fortunate, and to spread love and compassion wherever we go.

We as Christians celebrate his resurrection each year on Easter Sunday. We remember the message of love and forgiveness and the sacrifice he made for all humanity. We rejoice in the hope that his resurrection brings to our lives.

In this way, Easter becomes more than a holiday. It becomes a way of life, a reminder of the power of love to transform the world and make it a better place for all. It gives us hope for the future and proof of a promise kept.

Easter is celebrated all around the world as a time of renewal and a reminder that even in the darkest moments, there is always a chance for new life to emerge.

I pray that each of you will know the power of God's love and be reminded of it not only on this special day but also in all the days ahead. I don't know about you, but my story is only possible by God's amazing grace and the forgiveness he has given.

About the Author

Ashley Carter is a woman who wears multiple hats with grace and passion. As a loving wife, she cherishes the deep connection she shares with her spouse, offering support and creating a nurturing home environment. Ashley's dedication to her role as a mother is evident in her love and guidance, fostering growth and instilling values in her children.

Now as a doting grandmother, Ashley finds immeasurable joy in witnessing the growth and development of her grandchildren. Her warm presence and boundless affection create lasting memories for the younger generations to cherish.

Beyond her roles within her family, Ashley's heart lies in the realm of homesteading and writing. With a green thumb and a love for nature, she finds solace and inspiration in her garden. Tending to the plants and nurturing their growth allows her to connect with the earth and find peace in its beauty.

In addition to her green endeavors, Ashley is an inspirational writer. Through her words, she shares wisdom, insights, and uplifting messages with her readers. Her writings touch the hearts of many, encouraging them to embrace life's challenges and seek personal growth.

While Ashley's days are filled with family, garden work, and writing, she always makes time to prioritize what truly matters—spending precious moments with her loved ones. Whether it's a shared meal, a walk in nature, or simply sitting together and talking, these cherished moments are the heart and soul of Ashley's life. Her dedication to family and passion for her pursuits serve as an inspiration to all who have the privilege of knowing her.